The *Golden* Attitude

Beyond Positive Mental Attitude

———————

Thomas C Lux

The Golden Attitude

Copyright © 2009

By Thomas C Lux

Printed in USA

TCL Consulting Group

Motivation Concepts Publishing

Surprise, Arizona 85374

Orland Park, Illinois 60462

www.goldenattitude.com

ISBN 978-0-692-00614-6

Dedicated to my wife Lorie,

who is also my best friend and editor.

Thank you for your support and belief in me.

Contents

Prologue
THE GOLDEN ATTITUDE

Golden means a precious element, something valuable and Attitude means a predisposition to behave or think in a certain way.

Beyond Positive Mental Attitude

There is a tool that can help you through tough times and enable you to enjoy more good times in your life. I call it The Golden Attitude. When I was a boy I had this recurring dream. It was always a bright sunny day, early in the morning and I would get into a small silver single engine airplane. I would sit in the pilot's seat and the engine would start by itself, roll down the runway and slowly lift off the ground. I could control the height and direction of the plane with my thoughts. The plane would climb and turn in response to my thought, and I could view a beautiful distant world below. I felt exhilarated as I escaped the bonds of the earth. As the plane climbed higher my view expanded and from this loftier view everything looked clean and orderly. When viewed from this higher perspective everything seemed to slow down and any fears or concerns I had seemed to lessen and then vanish. After enjoying my flight of fantasy for a time it would occur to me I didn't know how to land the plane. Despite my anxious feelings the plane kept right on flying and eventually, without ever knowing how, I would manage to magically land the plane safely. Sometime the dream ended when I simply woke up from my dream in the middle of the flight, somewhat relieved since I was aware that I didn't know how to land the plane. I didn't know how my dream would end.

When I was a young man this dream changed and the airplane was replaced with a flying carpet which I could also control with my thoughts. It was one of those beautiful multi-colored, exotic, oriental carpets. The advantage of the flying carpet was its ability to go straight up or down and even hover motionless over any area I would choose. I could focus on a specific detail. I could slowdown or even stop to examine a point of interest. Again, I was high above the ground sitting on an open carpet and yet I always felt safe. I was in control of my flight with my thoughts. The magic carpet afforded a much more detailed view of the terrain. It was still always a beautiful bright sunny day. On the magic carpet, I could linger and savor any scene I could dream. I enjoyed and cherished these dreams but did not begin to understand their message for many years.

Today I realize that my thoughts can change everything that I experience. Although I shared my recurring dreams with others I never thought of actually taking flying lessons in a real airplane. Thoughts and dreams must be acted upon to become reality and sometimes we receive help in unexpected ways from unexpected sources.

One birthday I received a thoughtful and unusual gift from my wife. She presented me with a letter from the local airport stating the first thousand dollars of private flying lessons had been paid for and I should contact them for an appointment for my first lesson. Imagine my surprise! My wife asked me, "Will you take the lessons?" I said, "Sure." She prodded, "When?" I said, "Soon." She asked, "How soon?" I hesitated a moment and then replied, "I'll call them right now." I called the airport and they said, "Can you come today? We have an airplane and an instructor available right now." Before the end of that clear sunny day in January I had completed my first three hours of instruction. Those first three hours were a lot more difficult than flying in my dreams and earning my private pilot's license was challenging and even fearful at times. It took me about a year to complete my instruction and pass the flight and written tests to earn the right to fly, take passengers and share my new world. It felt great to experience the accomplishment of mastering the skill to fly my own airplane.

In retrospect I can see that our world is shaped by the way we choose to see it. A positive, forward-looking attitude enables us to do wonderful things. Sometimes we have no idea how we can accomplish the things we dream, but if we trust the universe and move in the direction of our dreams it is amazing how much we can accomplish and how interesting our life can be.

Chapter 1
Beginnings of Golden Attitude

The earliest beginnings of what I now call, Golden Attitude germinated while reading the book <u>Success through a Positive Mental Attitude,</u> by Napoleon Hill and W. Clement Stone. One idea that was imprinted permanently as a result of reading that book was, "There is a way of finding a solution to any problem." I reduced this idea to a concise simple exercise. Here is the mental exercise.

1. Whatever happens tell yourself, "That's good!"

2. Ask yourself, "What's good about it."

3. Keep searching for the good until you find it.

Remember, every adversity carries with it the potential for equal or greater good.

Think of this mental exercise as a tool that is always available to be used in good times or bad. It's a method of squeezing the most good out of any situation. There is always something good to be realized in any problem. We often don't see the good because we are not looking for it. I convinced myself that whenever life presented me with a problem I could follow these steps and I would eventually find the good in it. Applying this tool to my problems served me well for many years and became a habit. I came to believe that only two things happen to us. One is good things happen and when good things don't happen I consider it a learning experience. I can't recall exactly when it happened but over the years the Golden Attitude mental exercise became more than a way to solve problems. It became a way of life for me. My thoughts about this became my beliefs, and after holding these beliefs for a time, they became my truth. My mantra became, "It's all good." It's my job to look for and find the good in every situation.

In my communication seminars, I make this statement: "The quality of your life is in direct proportion to the quality of your communication with yourself and others." I then ask my audience, "Which of these two is more important, communication with yourself, or Communication with others?"

Given time to reflect, most of the audience chooses communication with yourself. I agree because there is power in self talk, and the power that our thoughts and attitudes have, shapes our lives. The classic book, <u>Think and Grow Rich,</u> by Napoleon Hill, first published in 1937, explored countless examples of success based on the biblical statement, "As a man thinketh in his heart, so he is." The classic cassette tape, <u>The Strangest Secret,</u> by Earl Nightingale, produced in 1960, put it another way. According to the tape, "We become what we think about." This audio tape topped sales of more than a million copies, making it the first spoken word recording to achieve Gold Record status. This recording is still readily available today in audio tape or CD format. In 2006 Rhonda Byrne produced a book and DVD, entitled <u>The Secret,</u> which dramatized the concept of "The Law of Attraction." The DVD contains comments from, and interviews with, contemporary motivational authors and speakers. The Law of Attraction states, "That which is like unto itself is drawn." To quote Wikipedia, the free online encyclopedia,

The phrase Law of Attraction has been used by many esoteric writers, although the actual definition varies greatly.

Most authors associate the Law of Attraction with the saying, "like attracts like", usually as applied to the mental life of human beings: that a person's thoughts (conscious and unconscious), emotions, beliefs and actions attract corresponding positive or negative experiences. This process has been described as "harmonious vibrations of the law of attraction", or "you get what you think about; your thoughts determine your experience.

My own life experiences have shown that often this law of attraction seems very real and other times it appears simply to be wishful thinking. It seems to work some of the time, yet does not seem to work all of the time. Part of me wants to accept the law of attraction and part of me questions the way it works. This law of attraction is often rejected by those applying strictly scientific standards. Dr. Carl Jung explained this sometime attraction between thoughts and events with the word, "Synchronicity." Jung described synchronicity as a pattern of connection that cannot be explained by conventional cause and effect reasoning. Jung introduced the concept as early as the 1920s.

I observe many of the effects that self-talk and thinking has on life experiences. I have gathered stories to share which exemplify these effects. I invite you to decide what might be valuable and useful. Choose whatever appeals and might appear helpful to you, and feel free to reject them. Life offers many choices, things we desire and things we don't. Choose what you want and focus only on what you want. Developing and practicing the Golden Attitude will enable you to do so consistently. Whenever faced with adversity, keep asking yourself, "What's good about this."

My earliest use of the Golden Attitude happened when I was a young salesman. I had a territory made up of small accounts that consisted mainly of customers that the senior salespeople didn't want. Sometimes when I called on the addresses listed on the books, not only was the account out of business, sometimes the buildings were even torn down. When I did find the business and called on them, they complained about not being called on by anyone from our company for years. I applied the Golden Attitude and said the words,

"That's good." Then I asked myself, "What's good about it?" First I appreciated the fact that at least I had some active accounts to call on and didn't have to rely on only cold calls to businesses that never even heard of our company. Then I realized that their complaints were an opportunity to allow me to make relationships better by showing my interest and concern. I soon learned that complaints presented me with opportunities to set myself apart as someone who cared about them and their problems. I realized that every time I responded to their problems, I endeared myself to them as a valuable resource. They would turn to me with many of their future problems or questions and that afforded me the opportunity to help them. That help often took the form of writing orders. I came to relish any complaint as a door opener to show the customer my knowledge and helpfulness. Eventually this became the centerpiece of my sales presentation. I even invited them to call me with any problem that was related to our industry and pointed out to them, that although I was relatively new in the business, I had resources of many experienced professionals within my company. I offered to help them get the answers they needed. Many of these inquiries turned to orders, but more importantly, I came to be regarded by them, and eventually by my industry, as a most knowledgeable resource. I consider the Golden Attitude responsible for my subsequent rise to Sales Manager and eventually to Vice President of Sales and Marketing with that company.

Chapter 2

How and why Golden Attitude works.

My business associate and friend, Jack Stanley, and I were sitting in our respective homes watching an educational television program at the same time. We were not aware that the other was watching the same program at the same time in cities a thousand miles apart. As the program started, a moderator told a group of about twenty people they were about to watch a film. Before showing the film the audience was told that they were about to take part in a test to measure their observation skills. The film depicted six basketball players, three wearing yellow uniforms and three others wearing blue. The players in yellow uniforms had a basketball and, during the film, they passed it to one another. The audience members were asked to watch the film closely and count the number of times the basketball players in yellow uniforms passed the basketball to another team member. Halfway through the film, a man dressed in a gorilla suit slowly walked into the scene. He sauntered through the players, stopped momentarily in front of the camera and beat his chest. Then he walked off. At the end of the film, a moderator asked, "Did you spot the gorilla?" Most people in the experiment looked confused because they completely missed seeing the gorilla. Most of the people did count the correct number of passes between the basketball players in the yellow uniforms. The few that saw the gorilla usually were off count on the passes. I found this hard to believe, since I couldn't understand how anyone could miss the obvious gorilla. Then they showed the film again. The reactions of the participants were disbelief. A few simply refused to believe their eyes. Weeks later I learned that Jack and I saw the same film at the same time and Jack did not see the gorilla and got the number of passes correct. Jack was totally committed to getting the answer right. His focus was on seeing the basketball passes. I watched the film but wasn't counting or focused on only the basketball players with yellow uniforms. The perceptual phenomenon of not seeing the gorilla is referred to as "inattentional blindness." It seems the human brain is amazingly good at detecting what it wants to find and completely overlooks other things that it is not looking for. The participants were so focused on counting the passes that they didn't see the gorilla. This may be hard to understand, but true.

Similarly when you are hungry, your brain focuses on finding food. When you are thirsty, it looks for something to drink. The problem is your brain can become so focused on seeing what it expects to see, it misses things that are obvious but unexpected.

Often when we have problems we focus on the problem and many times that's all we can see. When we use the Golden Attitude as a tool to change our focus from the problem to seeing only solutions or good things, it is amazing what we can find. It's not that problems aren't real; it's our "inattention" to the solutions that causes our blindness. So the question becomes, what are you looking for? Where is your attention focused? Whatever you focus on is probably more of what you will see and more of what will show up in your life. If you would like to investigate these studies, I suggest checking one well known study demonstrating "inattentional blindness" conducted by Daniel Simmons of the University of Illinois at Champaign/Urbana and Christopher Chabris of Harvard University.

If you choose to develop the habit of applying the Golden Attitude you will be training your brain to recognize the good things that surround you all the time. If you don't give your attention to something, you can become blind to its existence.

Another example is when a new mother comes home from the hospital and she is soon overwhelmed with the new tasks motherhood brings. She goes to sleep exhausted and manages to sleep through every imaginable noise until the baby cries. She hears the cry of her baby from the room down the hall and is instantly awake and alert. Most mothers in our audience start nodding their head and report a similar incident that happened to them. A few fathers chime in with similar experiences.

While we were in Arizona, my wife bought a turquoise van thinking it to be an unusual color. It's a color she never noticed before. Then all of a sudden she noticed turquoise vans everywhere. She assumed it must be a popular color in Arizona. When we returned to Chicago, guess what? Turquoise vans were everywhere.

A young couple opts to buy a house near the airport to save $50,000 compared to similar houses away from the noise of the airport. After they move in and they hear the noise of planes taking off overhead often, they begin to doubt the wisdom of their decision. However, thirty days latter, you may have guessed it, they don't even notice the jet noises anymore.

Some people have difficulty waking up early in the morning. But then they plan a vacation and they are really looking forward to the trip. The problem is they will have to get up at 4 AM to get to the airport in time to catch an early flight. They set three alarm clocks and arrange for a friend who works the night shift to give them a wake-up call. Then what happens? They somehow find themselves awake two minutes before the alarms go off. Did it ever happen to you?

These examples are explained by the part of our brain called the reticular activating system, (RAS). This is the part of your brain that automatically filters out information that isn't important to you, and brings to your attention things that are. The job of the RAS is to screen all incoming messages and choose what information should get the attention of the

23

conscious mind. Think of your RAS as the gatekeeper of your mind. It connects with the major nerves in the spinal column and brain. It sorts all the impulses that assault the brain each second, allowing only the most important through to alert the mind. Without the RAS, your mind could not function. It would be on overload. It has been estimated that a hundred million impulses assault the brain each second. What happens to them? When these impulses are registered in our brain, we begin to allow ourselves to be conscious of what we are feeling. Sometimes we do not become conscious of much of the incoming energy until later. Some of this gets stored in our subconscious mind and may show up at any time in a sudden realization or unexpected awareness. Often, at a later date, when we are engaged in a totally non-related activity, all of a sudden we have a realization, an "a-ha!" moment.

There are four main categories that focus the attention of the RAS

1. Physical needs
2. Self-made choices
3. Novelty
4. Your name

The first category, physical needs, seems obvious. As mentioned earlier, when you're hungry, your brain focuses on finding food. When you are thirsty, it looks for liquid. You are more likely to notice a restaurant when you are hungry, just as you're more likely to notice a gas station when you're running low on gas.

Having goals are a great example of the second category, Self-made choices. Many goal-setting programs point out that setting a goal can activate your RAS. Your mind has only one focus of attention at a time. If I ask you not to think about pink elephants, think about any elephant except pink ones, you cannot think about any other color elephant until you make yourself stop thinking about pink ones and change your current thought to an elephant of another color. Therefore, most goal-setting programs become quite structured and elaborate. The structure and suggestions, including affirmations, are designed to get the attention of your RAS and to program it to aid you in achieving your goal. We are asked to always keep our new "self-made choice" in our consciousness. Many life coaches ask us to be aware of all areas of their lives at once, and to try to find a balance in all of the areas. It quickly becomes clear that this is a daunting task. Some suggested areas often include Career, Money, Health, Family and Friends, Significant Other, Spirituality, Personal Growth, Fun and Recreation. No wonder it becomes a daunting task to try to keep all of this in our conscious awareness for improvement.

The third category, novelty, makes it hard to stay focused on our goals in today's world. Our minds are being continually bombarded with new and novel experiences. Television, the Internet, the presentation of commercials all force our minds to perceive and interpret quickly. The presentation of commercial products continues at an unprecedented pace. Television, color catalogs, internet pop up ads, new car commercials, and store offerings flood our minds with objects, wants, desires and wishes. Everything is presented in sound bites and our minds have been conditioned to process in microseconds.

So how can we influence our RAS to assist us in achieving our "self-made choices" in all areas of our lives? My answer is The Golden Attitude. Once you adopt it and apply it to the many areas of your life, you'll be focusing on what's good in all areas of your life and your RAS will be actively looking for more good things. (No pink elephants, just more good things.) Many people, without realizing it, have a positive attitude in some areas of their lives and a negative attitude in others. For example, some are very positive about their work and careers and negative when it comes to health and exercise. Others may be positive about their spirituality and negative about money. The combinations are endless. On the other hand, if you decide to apply the Golden Attitude to all areas of your life, think how you could see or find the good in all aspects of your life. Not only can you find solutions to your problems, your good times will take on greater value and be more appreciated.

Consider the fourth category, your name. Did you ever notice if someone calls out your name, you instinctively turn around to see who called your name? So before you go through the ritual of the Golden Attitude, start your thought process or self-talk using your own name to get the undivided attention of your RAS. For example, "OK Tom" (or whatever your name is), "We're going to apply the Golden Attitude to this."

Here is the mental exercise.

1. *Whatever happens tell yourself, "That's good!"*

2. *Ask yourself, "What's good about it."*

3. *Keep searching for the good until you find it.*

Remember, every adversity carries with it the potential for equal or greater good.

Chapter 3

Give it a test

In her book, <u>Feel the Fear and Do it Anyway</u>, Dr. Susan Jeffers states, "Negative words spoken to ourselves weaken us. Positive words spoken to ourselves strengthen us." To substantiate these claims Dr Jeffers performs a simple arm test. First she has a student in her class repeat the words, "I am a weak and unworthy person" ten times out loud. The student is then asked to extend her dominant arm parallel to the floor and resist her pushing it down. The student exhibits a weakness that easily allowed their arm to be pushed, down to their side, almost effortlessly. Next she has the same student repeat the words, "I am a strong and worthwhile person" ten times out loud. The student now exhibits strength and is able to resist the downward pressure and her arm remains rigidly straight, parallel to the floor. She goes on to write that it doesn't matter if the student believed the words to be true or not. Merely speaking the words repeatedly sent a message to the subconscious mind and caused weakness or strength in their arms. In my seminars I ask participants to volunteer for similar experiments in front of the group. I promise the volunteers that they will not be embarrassed and that they will gain a great deal more by participating than by just being an observer. Once the first person volunteers others follow quickly. After completing the spoken word test outlined above with similar results, I expand the test by asking the participants to think of tasks they really do well in their work, tasks that they enjoy, I ask them try to recapture how that feels to them. I ask them to be there mentally and feel that feeling. I tell them to think about it and recall how that feels. I then do the arm test and they test strong. Next I ask them to think of tasks that they perform poorly or don't enjoy doing and recall how that feels to them. As expected when I repeat the arm test they test weak. The participants never divulge the tasks to me or the audience; but merely dwell on the thoughts and feelings they associate with those tasks. The same type of process is repeated with thoughts and feelings associated with succeeding or failing in school or athletic endeavors. The results are always the same, "Positive thoughts, engender strong arms, and negative thoughts, weak ones.

So what do these tests tell us? Our self talk and inner thoughts are accepted by our inner self as true for us. Our inner self only acts on what it receives. Powerful words make us physically strong. Weak words make us physically weak.

How do you respond to life events in your self talk?

Something is a problem or... it's an opportunity.

Things are not my fault or ... I take total responsibility for my life.

Life's a struggle or ... Life's an adventure.

Something is terrible or... It's a learning experience.

What's wrong? or... What's good?

The first response is negative... The second response is positive. The message is clear. Stop feeding yourself Negative Thoughts and start feeding yourself Positive Thoughts. Why is this so important? The answer is the mind cannot distinguish between something that is real and something which is vividly imagined. To illustrate this consider the lemon story. I ask my students to close their eyes and imagine that they are standing in their kitchen in their home in front of their refrigerator. I continue my directions to them: "In your mind's eye see as much detail about your surroundings as you can. In a moment I will ask you to open the refrigerator, but before you do let me tell you what to expect. You will find the refrigerator empty except for one large, very yellow lemon. Okay, open the door now and see this very yellow lemon. Pick it up and notice how cold and waxy it feels. Take a sharp knife and cut it in half. Bring one of the halves closer to your face and see the drops of lemon juice oozing from its yellow pulp. Squeeze it gently and smell its fragrance as you bring it to your mouth and bite down into it sucking the bitter lemon juice with your tongue before you swallow it." The majority of the participants have a puckering reaction to the imaginary lemon; Their minds have a hard time distinguishing between a real and an imaginary lemon.

There is another often mentioned test involving basketball players practicing free throws. Three groups of players were tested on the percentage of Free Throws they were able to make. The results are recorded in the percentage of Free Throws made compared to the number of attempts they made. The first group then practiced free throws in the gym for one hour every day for thirty days. The second group practiced in their imagination for one hour a day for thirty days. As a control the third group was asked not to practice at all for thirty days. At the end of the thirty days the three groups were retested. The first and second group showed an improvement of 25% plus. The third group showed no improvement. The experiment showed almost no difference between the players that actually practiced and those who used only their imagination to practice.

Consider this excerpt from a report published on the Internet by Scott D. Williams, Ph.D., Department of Management, Raj Soin College of Business, Wright State University, Dayton, OH:

Is Imagined Practice More Helpful Than Actual Practice? Tasha Butts is executing one of the toughest shots in the sport of basketball, and mentally rehearsing such a performance beforehand can be very helpful. Butts is a guard on the University of Tennessee's basketball team. Sunday night, in the last second of Tennessee's post-season tournament game against Baylor, Butts was sent to the free throw line with a chance to win the game. There was a lot of pressure on her to perform. If she failed, her team might well have been eliminated from the tournament. Such pressure makes free throw shooting at the end of a basketball game very difficult. Butts succeeded and Tennessee defeated Baylor.

How should we prepare for difficult performances in athletics, the workplace, or other situations? Research has found that a combination of "imagined practice" and actual practice often results in better performances than those achieved with preparation that relies solely on actual practice. In addition to athletics, studies have shown that imagined practice improves performance in diverse contexts that include communication, education and clinical and counseling psychology. [1. Neck, C. P., Nouri, H., Godwin, J. L. (2003).*

"How self-leadership affects the goal-setting process." <u>*Human Resource Management Review*</u>, *13(4): 691-707.]*

Chapter 4

Choices and the flow of energy

One of your greatest powers is the power to choose your thoughts and words. Through your conscious mind you can choose to think positive thoughts with positive energy or you can choose negative thoughts with negative energy. When we choose to think about or verbalize our weakness or our unworthiness, we can measure the effect with the arm test. Why? The detailed explanation, of course, is more complex, but for our purposes let's consider a simplified explanation that is useful. The decision made by our conscious mind is sent to our subconscious mind. The subconscious mind doesn't judge our instructions; it simply carries out the instructions it is given. It does this by directing our internal energy through emotions and intellect and through an external universal flow of energy.

Let's examine the negative flow first. The negative thought, is selected by our conscious mind, sent to our subconscious and from there it is sent to our internal body where it is manifested as weakness in our arm strength. Other manifestations of negative thoughts might include blushing, sweating, nausea, forgetting knowledge we know when taking a test, feelings of incompetency, or simply a bad feeling in our gut. All these reactions seem to be uncontrollable but were actually set in motion by the choice of the conscious mind sending messages to the subconscious mind which merely obediently carried out the received messages.

Now let's explore some examples of how thoughts can result in an external universal flow of energy. Have you ever wondered how a dog seems to sense our fear, or how a horse seems to know that we are uncomfortable and feeling out of control when riding the horse for the first time? Consider the exchange of information between two people. In my seminars, I ask participants, if they heard two guest speakers and then they were told that one was extremely successful in many areas of his life while the other had failed in many areas of his life, could they tell the difference between the two if they listened to each guest speaker for 15 minutes or more. Most people felt they would be able to identify the successful guest speaker. These are examples of communicating through the flow of external universal energy, through non-verbal cues. Most seminar participants felt they would have the same ability to sense the difference between an extremely fearful person and a confident individual.

Research regarding female roommates in college dorms has shone that menstrual periods become synchronized after living in close proximity for extended periods of time. Current thinking attributes these events as possible communication by the transmission of messages through pheromones. I'm not suggesting what the method of communication is in this example, I am just suggesting that we may communicate in ways we don't yet completely understand. The exchange of external universal energy is one possible explanation. Remember the most important communication is the communication you have with yourself. It's just as easy to look for the good in every situation as it is to look for the bad. Why wouldn't anyone choose to seek the good especially if their seeking will enable them to find their highest good? Why would anyone want to dwell on the negative if there were any chance of that attracting more negativity? In her national bestseller, Positive Energy, Dr. Judith Orloff, M.D. states:

A basic dynamic of energy is that we attract who we are – the more positive energy we give off, the more we'll magnetize to us. Ditto for negativity. It works like this: Love attracts love. Grumpiness attracts grumpiness. Passion attracts passion. Rage attracts rage. The explanation: We are all subtle energy transmitters. We are constantly sending out signals that others on similar frequencies pick up on and gravitate toward – an instinctual call we may not be aware of. Why opportunities do or don't show up in our lives is a function of this.

Another fascinating report on this exchange of energy in Dr. Orloff's book states:

While working at a UCLA parapsychology lab, I was fascinated to discover an invisible anatomy to relationships. We were using Kirlian photography to measure energy fields by putting a finger or other objects on a light-sensitive plate. The energy auras we recorded looked like astonishing rainbows.

The first time I saw an aura, I was awed; it shot off the edge of someone's fingertip like a flame of a magnificent white fire. My work focused on measuring the aura of plants and how they interacted with humans. One day an arrogant Ivy League psychiatrist visited the lab. It was immediately evident that his purpose was to put our work down. Thus we wickedly decided to use our research to show him something about himself. First we measured the boundaries of a leaf's energy field on a Kirlian plate. Then we asked the psychiatrist to place his index finger beside it. Startled, he watched as the corona of the leaf recoiled and shrunk to half its original size. Wow. The leaf's sentiments about this psychiatrist matched our own. As with leaves, so with people.

Judith Orloff, M.D., a psychiatrist and an energy expert, is an assistant clinical professor at UCLA. She is an international lecturer on the relationship of intuition, energy, and medicine. Her work was featured on NPR, CNN, and in USA Today.

Chapter 5

Seeking your highest good

Albert Einstein once said the most important question a human being can ask is, "Is the universe friendly?" Einstein didn't say the universe was or wasn't friendly; he said it was the most important question a human being can ask. If you think the universe is truly friendly and supportive of you, this obviously will affect your attitudes and expectations. Of course the same applies if you think the universe is not friendly. When you decide that the universe is friendly, your positive outlook is likely to be mirrored by positive responses from others. On the other hand, if you are fearful of the universe, your life will likely seam like a series of disappointments. It is what you choose to believe that is critical.

I stopped at a sandwich shop recently and ordered a glass of water with my sandwich. I was handed a paper cup and directed to the soft drink dispenser and told to press the little lever marked water. This was the first time I saw the lever marked in two languages. One was water and the other was agua. It occurred to me that water is the same no matter what word we use to describe it. A quick trip to the internet revealed that water in German would be wasser, in French eau, in Italian acqua and in Swahili maji. The water doesn't change because we call it by another name. When we make our choice about the friendliness of the universe, some people would like to use a different word instead of universe. Religious people might prefer to say God; others might say First Cause, The Creator, Supreme Being, or Source Energy. Whatever you call that power or entity, it is important to decide if it is friendly. Is it for you or against you? Getting back to the water button, no matter what word you use to describe water, once you push the button, water flows and fills up your cup until you release the button. We expect the water to flow and if we want to we could keep pushing the button and fill up a bottle, a pail, a washtub, or a bathtub. We take for granted the water will keep flowing and don't even question the source. Think of your good flowing from an inexhaustible source. I like to imagine the largest water tower I have ever seen, then imagine one a thousand times bigger, then imagine it is connected to a large lake reservoir which is constantly replenished by rain. Imagine this is our source for all good things and we are all connected so our good will flow to us like water as long as we keep our connection open. Our thoughts and attitudes keep the connections open and flowing or they cause the flow to be restricted. The choice is always ours. Whenever we experience anything in our life that appears undesirable, we can always look for another connection to our greater good. Remember, every adversity carries with it the potential for equal or greater good, if you keep searching for that greater good until you find it. Keep asking yourself what's good about the situation.

Let the Golden Attitude be your "GO TO" button. Keep pressing it until you find your highest good. I ask my seminar audiences if they can remember a time when something happened to them that seemed like a bad thing at the time it happened. But in retrospect it turned out to be good. Many recalled the incident, and realized that what seemed bad at the time actually was a good thing. Perhaps it was the best thing that could have happened because it led to events that actually turned out to be best in the long run. In other words, if the original event or situation didn't happen then, they wouldn't have been in a position to receive some important benefit. A new or better job, a new relationship or any numbers of good things in their life, seemed to flow from the original seemingly undesirable event. Think about your own life and I'm sure you will recall something similar. If you apply the Golden Attitude to these tough times, you can speed up the realization of all things working for good in your life. Practicing a Golden Attitude can help you to realize your highest good.

Chapter 6
Going with the flow

In goal setting workshops the importance of having a balanced life suggests we set goals in four main categories of our life.

SPIRITUAL - Psychological growth, worship, fulfillment
PHYSICAL - Health, fitness, weight, nutrition
FAMILY - Activities, priorities, relationships, friends, fun
CAREER - Position, recognition, income, budget, security

Goals provide a roadmap for our lives. However, while goal setting has helped me accomplish many things in my life, I can't help but notice that some of the most important and significant turning points in my life had nothing to do with goal setting. Significant unplanned events changed the direction of my life from time to time. My reaction to these events often determined the new directions in many areas of my life. Having acquired the habit of applying the Golden Attitude to most happenings, I was able to react favorably to these unplanned events. I was often able to see good in the apparent adversity. Participants in our workshops tell me they like the stories I tell to illustrate the lessons I have learned. Many say the stories teach the lesson better than my explanations. Therefore I want to share some of the stories which involve my use of the Golden Attitude.

My first story is a career story. After 26 years in corporate life I found myself in a situation where work was no longer fun. The company I worked at was acquired by a large conglomerate and the clash of cultures got to the point where I felt I needed to make a change. I decided to strike out on my own, forming a sales representative company in the same industry. After getting off to a grueling first year and a half my new company came into its own. I brought my oldest son into the business and we were enjoying increasing sales and earnings. Then one of the companies we represented who was our largest source of income suddenly called me in for an announcement. The General Manager announced they were discontinuing the use of sales representatives and were switching over to salaried fulltime salesmen. He told me that if all the reps did as well as we did they wouldn't be making this move. Some consolation! In one day over $100,000 of income was gone from my new company. After they finished delivering this news I sat quietly for a while and then the thought occurred to me to apply the Golden Attitude. That's good. I told myself. What's good about it? Before I left their office I found myself suggesting they consider my son for one of the new company salesman positions. As I drove onto the expressway ramp I kept telling myself it was good but couldn't get my stunned mind to come up with anything good. Still I felt relieved and even happy. It all didn't compute but I went with my feelings and kept challenging myself to ask the question, "What's good about it?" No answers were forthcoming. It did quickly turn out to be a great opportunity for my son. The company hired him and he has gone on to make a successful career on his own away from the shadow of his father. It still left me with a big hole in my income. I managed to stay positive despite not having a clue how I was going to replace the lost income. After about a month of searching for the good in this problem I finished an hour of quiet time trying to search for the good. While sitting quietly in my office the phone rang and a stranger called me out of the blue. He got my name from several people in my field as someone who could help them put a new business plan together for a new sales division they were contemplating. They also needed someone to design and implement a training program for their sales force. If I had gotten this call before I lost the income, I certainly would not have been interested since I was totally involved in growing my own new successful company. Now I was free to consider the new proposition. After some negotiating I chose to hire on as a consultant. My career was off in a new direction. This change in my work proved to be more rewarding and opened my life to a whole new chapter. Thanks to the Golden Attitude I was looking for some new good to come out of this seeming adversity and the universe delivered it to me. In this situation I applied the tool of the Golden Attitude. Looking for the good was like planting a seed. This seed of imagination took time to germinate and sprout as well as grow and come to fruition. Applying the Golden Attitude doesn't always result in instant results, but if one keeps on applying the Golden Attitude one becomes aware of the opportunities that surround us all the time in this opulent universe. Conversely if we focus on the problem, we usually attract more of the same and miss opportunities or even reject them.

My second story is a combination Physical and Spiritual story. As part of a routine annual checkup my doctor recommended a stress test. The test went routinely with the doctor stating everything seemed normal but he was going to have the results sent to a specialist for evaluation. Later that week I got a phone call from the nurse asking me to come in to discuss my test results. It seems that the specialists that read my test results had noticed something that wasn't right and suggested that I have an angioplasty done to check it out. I was reluctant to have an invasive test done and stated my preference not to have the test unless it was absolutely necessary. My doctor encouraged me to have the test in light of some of the symptoms of rapid heart beats that occurred occasionally. Still he said the decision was mine but he strongly encouraged me to have the tests and find out exactly what was going on. He stated without the test there was no other way we could really know what was going on. After several more episodes of a rapid heartbeat I was still reluctant to have the invasive test with the risks they presented. Looking back, I understand now that I was giving in to fear. Then one Sunday I was attending a church service and one of the board members was substituting for the vacationing minister and gave a talk on being open to receiving our good. He recounted how he had lost his position as an accountant for a firm he worked for for ten years. It seemed the business had merged and the new management felt they needed someone who had more education and greater accounting skills. He talked about accepting what had happened and he was in the process of looking for his higher good in this event. He went on to say he had already found his new job with a new company which had less travel time and more benefits and a greater salary. The thought occurred to me that he was practicing the Golden Attitude. I met with him after the service and told him his story had inspired me. It reminded me about my Golden Attitude and how I was failing to apply it to a health issue I was currently facing. He smiled broadly and calmly reassured me that he had a strong feeling everything would work out for my highest good. He encouraged me to have the test. It was just what I needed to nudge me into the decision to go ahead and have the test done as soon as possible. Somehow before the test I had what I refer to as a "knowing" that everything would work out fine. It turned out that the test revealed a blockage in the diagonal artery of my heart. This is a small artery in the left front lower region of the heart. They were able to place a stint at the same time they did the inspection with the angioplasty. The other good news was that all my other arteries were clear. This artery got clogged because it was genetically smaller than they would expect in a heart of my size. At the time they placed an uncoated stint because a coated stint wasn't available in the small size. Since then problems reported with coated stints indicate getting an uncoated stint was a good thing. The doctor also stated that if left unnoticed and untreated my condition would have probably caused a heart attack. What a reminder to apply the Golden Attitude to apparent problems.

My third story is a combination Spiritual and Family story. It is by far the greatest test of the Golden Attitude that I have ever encountered in my entire life. It's hard to begin writing about it even after many years have passed. A routine

Chest X-Ray taken at an immediate care center showed a dark spot on my wife's lung near the area adjacent to her wind pipe. She was immediately referred to a specialist at the local hospital and the worst fear was confirmed; inoperable lung cancer. Radiation was begun immediately followed by chemotherapy. Our lives changed immediately and dramatically. We talked and agreed we would stay optimistic and pursue every possible avenue to get the disease into remission. At first the radiation shrunk the tumor to the point it seemed to disappear. The chemo was then completed and her doctor said he was unable to see any sign of the cancer. She appeared to be in remission. After several months her symptoms of tiredness returned and the doctor confirmed the cancer was back. More treatments were just slowing the spread and fourteen months after her original diagnosis she made a very peaceful transition and died. During those fourteen months we became closer than we were for all of our 24 years of marriage. In the last month I was totally involved in her care on a 24/7 basis. I struggled through the funeral and stayed busy attending to all sorts of details including the creation of a memorial book consisting of letters of remembrance from family and friends. The last thing I had to take care of was the placing of her headstone. Her epitaph was her message to all of us: "Love one another." After that I became despondent and about a month later I had a full blown panic attack. I actually believed I was having a heart attack and was going to die. A quick trip to the hospital and a complete check revealed no physical health problems and a diagnosis of extreme stress. Several months passed before I remembered to use the Golden Attitude tool. I choked on the thought, my wife died and there is good in there somewhere. My whole body trembled. How could I even allow myself to think that? Eventually I was able to ask myself what could possibly be good about the death of my wife. It took several months before I was able to seriously look for the good in her passing. The answers came slowly at first. Her pain and sickness had ended. Being as active and fun loving as she was her decline in health and vitality had been extremely difficult for her. Now she was at peace. I remembered a time when she was asked, "Aren't you angry that you got incurable cancer and others who smoked did not?" Her reply was, "Who should I be angry at? Many people encouraged me to stop and the dangers are clearly printed in every pack of cigarettes." I remembered a time when she said, "I'm not afraid to die, I'm sure God has a place for me in heaven." She told me a story she had once heard about twins talking to each other in their mother's womb. One twin was talking about leaving the womb and looking forward to new adventure in the world beyond the safety of their mother's womb. "I wonder what it will be like out there; what great new adventure awaits us?"

The other twin replied, "Are you crazy? Outside the womb, nothing awaits us. It will be the end of us. We will cease to exist, away from the nourishment of our mother." If she were a twin I'm sure she would have been the first one out.

Almost everyone enjoys butterflies, but few people stop to think that the beginning for the butterfly is the end for the caterpillar. The story of the dragonfly is even more thought provoking. They lay their eggs in water or mud which hatch within one to three weeks into larvae. The larvae molts eight to twelve times before becoming a dragonfly. It spends its time crawling around in the mud anywhere from two to four years depending on the species. Then one day it crawls from the mud out of the water onto a plant and emerges as an adult dragonfly. It must rest and dry in the sun so that its wings can stiffen and harden before it can fly. Then in an instant it can fly. Immediately it can fly forward, backwards and even hover in one spot like a helicopter. No practice, no learning, it just knows. The dragonfly flies away from the water and makes its way back when it is ready to find a mate and breed, beginning the life cycle once again. The process of transforming from larvae to adult, called metamorphosis, often symbolizes rebirth. My wife liked to wear her silver dragonfly pin. What I came to learn was that her death had nothing to do with me. It was about her life which in my view had apparently ended but for her was just a transition to a new realm. My life on earth was still to be lived.

Chapter 7
Infinite possibilities

The universe is infinite. We live in a universe of infinite possibilities for good. However, if we see ourselves as victims, we don't bother to look for our good. Only when we accept things as they are can we ask, "What is the next best thing to do right now?" Then we must listen with the expectancy of receiving our good. Wherever we are on our journey of life it is well to remember there is always more. Life is a matter of "gradually becoming." Things take time. When we expect fast, easy answers, we are often disappointed. Life unfolds when we persist or as I like to say, "Keep going until you get there." I have some stories to illustrate these concepts: "gradually becoming" and "keep going until you get there."

The earliest example I recall in my life concerns learning how to swim. When I was old enough to go to the public park swimming pool by myself, I observed kids swimming and diving off both the low boards and the high dive platform and having great summer fun. There were no classes so I had to teach myself. I started by doing a dog paddle in shallow water. Then I cautiously stayed close to the rail on the side of the pool. I paddled to a depth I knew was over my head. I always stayed within arm's reach of the rail. As my confidence grew I started jumping into the deeper water from the side of the pool, coming up, and dog paddling to the rail. Convinced I had mastered that, I started diving into deep water and paddling to the rail. Next came jumping off the low diving board, followed by diving off of it. After that came the high board. It was 10 ft high, but seemed like 20 from my young perspective. Many climbed the ladder only to climb back down without jumping off. I remember going out to the edge and then letting others go ahead of me while I thought it over and worked up my courage. I don't remember climbing down the ladder without jumping off, but I may have. After mastering the jump came the final goal, diving off the high board. There was a lot of letting others go ahead of me before the first dive. I can still remember the moment of truth. Mustering up my courage, I stood on the edge of the board, looking down to the water below. Finally, I pushed off into the unknown head first through the air. I broke the water and headed all the way down to the bottom of the pool. After touching the bottom, I pushed up to the surface and propelled myself two feet out of the water with a triumphant feeling of accomplishment. What a great feeling. It was a moment never to be forgotten. This has served as a metaphor for my life ever since. Life is a series of events that have us always becoming more and persisting through those changes until we get there, wherever we choose to go. This swimming story is important to me because it is my earliest experience of persisting and having it pay off in the realization of my goal. It is what I think about when I consider a new adventure or goal. Start slow, increase in increments, and keep going until you get there.

The next story is my Marathon Story. When I was promoted from salesman to sales manager I quickly became aware I needed to find an exercise program to offset my inactivity and stress of spending hours at my desk. A friend in Texas sent me an audio cassette tape with simple instructions on how to start a walking program. Find your most comfortable clothes and shoes, it said, and start walking in the largest open floor area in your home in the pattern of a figure eight. It explained that walking in figure eights allowed a right turn followed by a left turn which is much better than walking in circles so you don't get dizzy and fall down. How simple is that! The tape went on to say you should do it for whatever time is comfortable for you and then keep increasing the time at your own pace until you can do it for 20 minutes. When you're ready, and not before, take it outside. Walk ten minutes away from your house and ten minutes back. Gradually increase your walking time to 30 minute a day. At your own pace again increase the time gradually until you can walk 60 minutes.

For most people walking an hour will cover approximately 3 miles, more or less. I tried it and it worked. Starting in my family room I progressed to the three miles outside in 60 minutes. The next step was following Dr. Kenneth H. Cooper's aerobics program for walking and eventually running. Dr. Cooper is called the father of aerobics. He has an age related schedule which allows you to gradually increase your walking or running at a safe pace over a period of 14 to 18 weeks based on your age. For example, in his walking program for ages 40-49 in week one you start by doing 2 miles in 38 minutes, three times a week. Each week the schedule increases the distance or decreases the time. By week fourteen you are asked to walk 3 miles in 43 minutes four times a week.

After completing this schedule I was feeling comfortable and confident in my exercise program. Then the universe conspired to show me there was more. My primary motivation had been health and fitness: However one of my fellow workers had run the Boston Marathon and had encouraged a mutual friend to run the Chicago Marathon with him. I went downtown to support and encourage them. There was much excitement and enthusiasm in the crowd for all the runners. Then it happened. One runner, after having run 25 miles to the point where I was standing in the crowd, stopped, bowed to the applauding crowd and then did a back flip! He raised his arms high into the air, took another bow and ran off to finish the race. That really excited me. To see that display of human potential was inspiring.

I started to entertain the idea that I might run the marathon myself. I picked up a book on how to train for your first marathon. After reading the book, the idea that it was possible began to form in my mind. I started to follow the training over the following months. It took a lot of my time to train but I persisted and eventually registered for the race.

When the race day came I was nervous and excited. I didn't sleep well the night before. My son drove us downtown from our suburban home and then he went to positions along the route to record the event on film. He was there for the finish and the ride home. The race was exhilarating and I ran beyond my pace. I'm told this was normal because of all the released adrenaline. The crowds were wonderfully supportive the entire 26 miles cheering the runners on.

About twenty-two miles out, I hit the proverbial "wall." My muscles gave out and I felt as if I couldn't lift my leg another time. A short walk and changing the muscles I used allowed the spent muscles to recuperate and I went on to find a new source of energy I didn't think I had. After a mile of walking, I began to run again. Energy came up from some unknown reservoir deep within. The crowd's cheer grew louder, even though we were in the back of the pack. People always seem to love the underdogs. Their cheers nourished my soul and body. The end of the race was finally in sight, and new energy pumped up from even greater depths. I ran an even greater pace than normal. One final sprint to the finish, and a sense of elation rushed through my body as I crossed the finish line. I felt successful, complete and whole!

They say some spend days recovering from their first marathon. For me, everything returned to normal the next day. I often look back on that event. I am always glad I did it. I am always proud of my accomplishment, although I never ran another marathon. I learned that realizing your potential is a noble goal. Inspiration, hard work, and accomplishment are food for the soul. They are exhilarating. One of the important lessons of the marathon training program was persistence. When the training schedule called for ten, fifteen or twenty mile runs, it was normal to think you can't continue to the end of that mileage. The instructions were clear, commit to the mileage and don't quit. Keep going even if you have to walk, but finish the distance. These principles apply to many things in life. Just go for it. CONCEIVE, BELIEVE, AND ACHIEVE.

My next story is one of continuing education. When I was finishing high school I thought of going on to college to pursue a degree in engineering. Having observed my older brothers being drafted and sent off to Korea and Germany, respectively, I chose to enlist in the Army to get my service obligations behind me. Before leaving for the Army I squeezed in a couple of classes at a local community college, and after the service I continued to take a couple more classes before getting married and starting a family. My formal education ended then and my energies were consumed by career and family. Good intentions to go back to school to pursue a degree went dormant for years. Then at age 61, I took two classes at my local community college. I enjoyed it so much I trimmed my consulting schedule to allow me to go back to school full time the following semester. I registered for 19 credit hours that semester. Because I was now considered a full time student, I was required to take a mandatory class, called College 101. This class provided an opportunity to assess study strategies, set college and career goals, examine values and decision making skills, and develop an appreciation for diversity. My instructor was a woman my age who was widowed and recently remarried. I met her new husband who was 73 years old and was still teaching. In fact, he was teaching College 101 at the same school. I found that incredibly inspirational and decided that was something I would like to be able to do after retiring from the business world. I was working to complete an Associates Degree and I would need to get a Bachelors' Degree and then a Masters Degree in order to teach in community college. I successfully completed that semester and then got creative in my course choices by taking regular courses as well as online courses in order to complete my Associates Degree in less than two years. I started on my Bachelors' Degree at a university that operated on a trimester calendar. Three trimesters a year plus a program that allowed credit for my work experience sped up the process of gathering the necessary credits for my B.A. degree. In order to earn credit for my life experience I was required to submit a portfolio on each course that demonstrated mastery of the course material and documented work to substantiate my claim.

Because I was doing consulting work and training at this time I could utilize all my spare time to devote to working on my education. I was able to earn my Bachelors' Degree in less than two years and graduated at age 64. I immediately enrolled in graduate school at the same university. I added some weekend seminar classes and correspondent and video courses for extra credit hours and was able to complete the requirements of the degree Masters of Arts Communication and Training by the age of 65. I did my internship for my M.A. as a student teacher working with my mentor/professor teaching introductory classes to both undergraduate and graduate students in the College of Communications at Governors State University in Illinois. The following semester I was back at my community college teaching College 101 just as I had hoped to do. And that was just the beginning!

My university mentor/professor, Dr. Michael Purdy, invited me to create a class to help graduate students prepare for teaching at community colleges. He invited me to teach the course at Governors State University. In preparing for this class, I came to know the author, Dr. Richard E. Lyons, who wrote the textbook I chose for my new class. He became extremely interested in the progress of my new class as this was the first time his book had been used as a textbook. We communicated continually over the next year and then came a big surprise. Dr. Lyons informed me he had signed a contract to write a book entitled <u>Best Practices for Supporting Adjunct Faculty</u>. He invited me to write a chapter in his book about the class I had created and taught. In 2007 the book was published by Anker Publishing Company, Inc. Bolton, MA. My contribution to the book is Chapter 8 entitled, <u>An Applied Course in Teaching That Serves the Home and Neighboring Institutions.</u> Being a published author was not in my original plan. The universe just presented that possibility and viewing it as good allowed me to take advantage of that opportunity. You might say I kept going, incrementally until I got there. This was part of my "gradual becoming." Sometimes when I look back on this period of my life I wonder how I accomplished what I did in that amount of time. But back then, once I decided on my goal, circumstances and opportunities just seemed to present themselves. One must still choose, act, and persist, but when we seize an idea or perhaps when it seizes us, heaven and earth seem to move to make a way where there seemed no way. I felt joy on that journey. It all seemed so natural and obviously the right thing to do.

My last story took place in a matter of hours and yet in my mind it stands out as most significant. It remains a permanent life lesson not only for me but for other members of my family. My son was in high school and his first car was a really old International Harvester Scout with four wheel drive. When he found a newer model complete with a snow plow the old Scout was abandoned to a corner of the backyard while its fate was being contemplated. As the days turned into months, the old Scout became an irritation to the serenity of the landscape. When its fate had been decided and the day of departure came, an unexpected Chicago snowstorm dumped 10 inches of snow overnight. The drifts complicated our plan to have it towed away. The tow truck driver was reluctant to back into grass covered with snow. He was fearful that his truck would get stuck in the drifts. After some discussion I assured him that if the tow truck was unable to pull out the Scout, we could always unhook it and then we could push the truck out by hand by rocking it back and forth. The reluctant driver finally agreed. After hooking up to the Scout, everything started moving slowly and then the tow truck wheels started spinning in the deep snow drifts. We shoveled paths under the tires through the snow. We tried again, only to watch it sink deeper in the snow. We shoveled again with very little progress. I suggested we keep the tow truck hooked up to the Scout and my brother and I would push the tow truck and my son would push the Scout. We would rock the vehicles synchronized with the driver's application of the accelerator. Reluctantly they agreed to the new plan. My son was doubtful the plan would work; frankly I think we all were, but we were determined to give it a try. We all got behind the trucks and pushed again and this time I became the cheerleader. "One, two, three push. One, two, three push!" I shouted! timed to the surges of power. The whole hookup crept forward, inches at a time, but forward. The wheels grabbed and then spun. Agonizingly slow, we moved forward through the snow drifts. Eventually we made it to the freshly plowed street with one last surge of power. Once freed from the grips of the snow, the driver kept going and didn't slow down for another 50 yards before he came to a stop.

The story has grown and been retold and embellished by my family over the years and has become a symbol of what's possible. Whenever a family member suggests something can't be done, our response is, "Remember the Scout in the snow? Keep going until you get there!" Eventually we dropped the reference to the Scout or the snow and the phrase simply morphed into, "Keep going until you get there."

Chapter 8

Guidance for more

There is an old Cherokee tale about a battle that goes on inside of every person. It is said there is a battle between two wolves inside us all. One is evil. It is anger, envy, jealousy, sorrow, regret, greed, arrogance, self-pity, guilt, resentment, inferiority, lies, false pride, superiority and ego. The other is good. It is joy, peace, love, hope, serenity, humility, kindness, benevolence, empathy, generosity, truth, compassion, and faith." The question is "which wolf will win?" And the answer is, "The one you feed." When we feed ourselves with good thoughts we are guided unerringly to our highest good. That's where practicing the Golden Attitude keeps us on track sometimes to an outcome beyond our wildest dreams. The guidance is always present even when we ignore it completely. It remains always present, ready and waiting for us to begin again. When things go wrong we need only stop, think and get quiet. It is important to focus on what we want and not what's happening that we don't want. If we consistently declare the presence of good in all things and keep looking, we find the good we seek.

The last story I want to share with you in this book is how I met my wife Lorie. After one loses a spouse it seems a lot of people decide the best thing they can do for you is to "fix you up." Good intentioned friends and relatives scour their list of friends, relatives, social contacts and even friends of friends as well as business contacts to help you along. They also urge you to get out socially meeting with other people in similar situations, whether divorced or widowed. As a widower, I reviewed all suggestions from well meaning family and friends and I came to the conclusion that I was going to be alone for awhile so I needed to adjust to living by myself. Many spouses feel like they will never find another mate as well suited to them as the one they lost. It became clear to me that getting involved socially with a group of people in similar circumstances was a good idea but the chances of finding a compatible mate seemed remote, to say the least. In the Chicago area they have single dances sponsored by a group called "Good Time Charley Dances." I also found a group that sponsored outings of varied venues, such as plays, theatre, travel destinations as well as sporting events.   These organizations have value in their offerings of social contacts in a safe, friendly environment.   I soon realized that it was unlikely that I would find a new partner for life at any of these events.   Nonetheless, they did offer a social outlet for me as a single person.   Then one night when I planned to attend a dance, I was rather tired and decided not to go.   My son was surprised that I was cancelling out at the last minute and urged me to take a shower and go. He found that when one is least inclined to try again, to do so anyway, is precisely the time when things seem to turn out great.   I decided to go one more time. It so happened that my future wife, Lorie, was tired of going to these dances and was reluctant to go that night as well. She decided to go one more time at the urging of her friend. So it was that we both ended up meeting each other that night. From the time she accepted my invitation to dance we spent the rest of the night talking and dancing.   We both felt such a strong attraction to each other that we saw each other for the next ten days and decided after those ten days we would marry. We met in January and married in March and that was ten years ago. To quiet any concerns our children had we decided to get an iron clad prenuptial agreement drawn up and sent them a copy. They stopped asking; "What's the rush?"

Last year my son Jeff, a social worker in California, invited me to give a presentation to the Council of Nephrology Social Workers. It was a new audience for me but I was flattered that he asked me to speak. The session went very well and I was surprised by their urging me to write a book on Golden Attitude. Last year I started making my Golden Attitude presentation to another new group, the seniors who are members of Rio Institute for Senior Education, (RISE). RISE has a relationship with Rio Salado College in Surprise, Arizona. What an audience! They are experienced, intelligent, successful people who are still hungry for knowledge. I had the same requests for a book with this group. My accountant recently invited me to present to the CPA Association of Illinois. I am looking forward to presenting my seminar on Golden Attitude to more diverse groups. I have begun to accumulate stories from the members of my new varied audiences. I can see writing another book consisting of a collection of stories from readers. If you'd like to share your story or experience with me, send it to me at this email address: motivation@att.net. I look forward to hearing your Golden Attitude stories!

How To Have A Golden Attitude

1. *Whatever happens tell yourself, "That's good!"*

2. *Ask yourself, "What's good about it."*

3. *Keep searching for the good until you find it.*

<u>REMEMBER</u>

"Every adversity carries with it the
potential for equal or greater good."

www.ingramcontent.com/pod-product-compliance
Lightning Source LLC
Chambersburg PA
CBHW071949100426
42736CB00042B/2510